First Guide to Maps

Mapping the United States

**Marta Segal Block and
Daniel R. Block**

Heinemann Library
Chicago, IL

©2008 **Heinemann Library**
a division of Reed Elsevier Inc.
Chicago, Illinois

Customer Service 888-454-2279
Visit our website at **www.heinemannlibrary.com**

Designed by Jennifer Lacki, Kimberly R. Miracle, and Betsy Wernert

Illustrations by Mapping Specialists

Originated by Modern Age

Printed and bound in China by South China Printing Co. Ltd.

12 11 10 09 08
10 9 8 7 6 5 4 3 2 1

10-digit ISBNs: 1-4329-0793-X (hc); 1-4329-0799-9 (pb)

Library of Congress Cataloging-in-Publication Data

Block, Marta Segal.
Mapping the United States / Marta Segal Block and Daniel R. Block.
    p. cm. -- (First guide to maps)
Includes bibliographical references and index.
ISBN-13: 978-1-4329-0793-8 (hc)
ISBN-13: 978-1-4329-0799-0 (pb)
1. Cartography--United States--Juvenile literature. 2. United States--Maps--Juvenile literature. I.
    Block, Daniel, 1967- II. Title.
GA405 .B562008
912.73--dc22

2007048623

Acknowledgments
The author and publishers are grateful to the following for permission to reproduce copyright
material: ©Jupiter Images p. **27** (Comstock); ©Map Resources p. **4**; ©Corbis p. **26** (Hulton-Deutsch
Collection); ©USGS pp. **5**, **18** (Courtesy Maptech).

Cover image reproduced with permission of ©Getty Images/NPA.

Every effort has been made to contact copyright holders of any material reproduced
in this book. Any omissions will be rectified in subsequent printings if notice is given
to the publisher.

Disclaimer
All the Internet addresses (URLs) given in this book were valid at the time of going to press.
However, due to the dynamic nature of the Internet, some addresses may have changed, or sites
may have changed or ceased to exist since publication. While the author and publisher regret any
inconvenience this may cause readers, no responsibility for any such changes can be accepted by
either the author or the publisher.

Contents

Any words appearing in the text in bold, **like this**, are explained in the glossary.

What Are Maps?

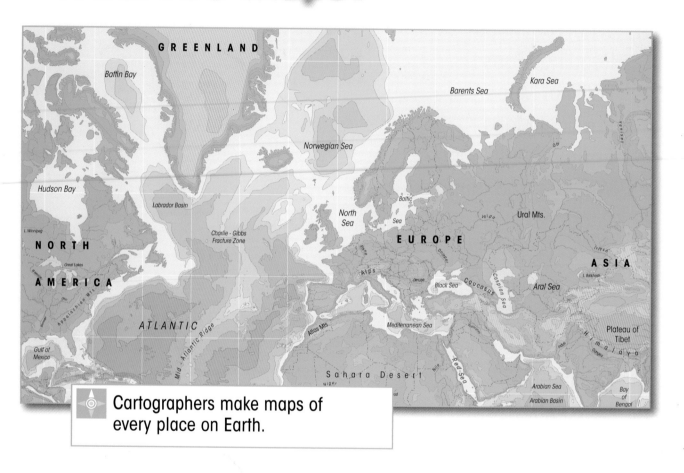

GREENLAND

Baffin Bay

Kara Sea

Barents Sea

Norwegian Sea

Hudson Bay

Labrador Basin

North
Sea

Baltic
Sea

Ural Mts.

L. Winnipeg

Charlie - Gibbs
Fracture Zone

EUROPE

ASIA

NORTH

Great Lakes

L. Balkhash

AMERICA

Alps

Danube

Aral Sea

Black Sea

Caucasus

Caspian Sea

Appalachian Mts.

ATLANTIC

Mid - Atlantic Ridge

Atlas Mts.

Mediterranean Sea

Plateau of
Tibet

Gulf of
Mexico

Himalaya

Sahara Desert

Nile

Red Sea

Niger

Arabian Sea

Bay
of
Bengal

Arabian Basin

Cartographers make maps of every place on Earth.

A map is a flat drawing of a part of the world. People who make maps are called **cartographers**.

Maps are a good way to learn about the place where you live. They show the location of states and cities. They show natural features of the land. They show how people use the land.

This map shows the shape of the land in North America.

Reading Maps

Maps have many **symbols**. Symbols are small pictures or shapes that stand for things in real life. Maps have a **key** that tells what the symbols on the map mean.

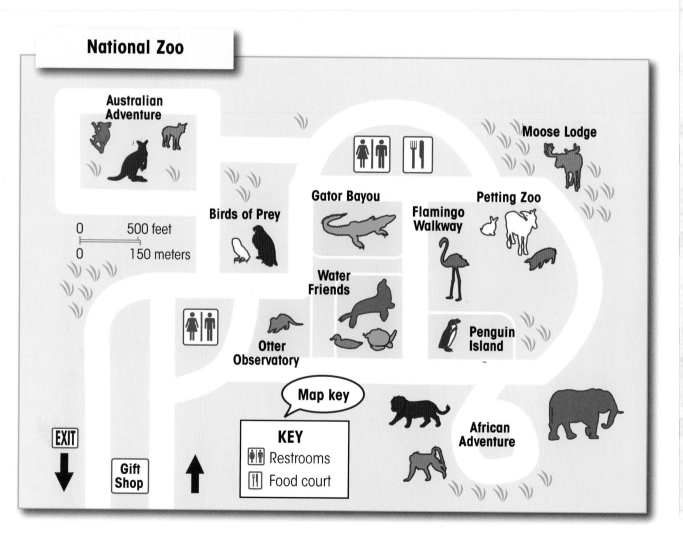

National Zoo

Australian Adventure

Moose Lodge

Gator Bayou

Petting Zoo

Flamingo Walkway

Birds of Prey

0   500 feet
0   150 meters

Water Friends

Otter Observatory

Penguin Island

Map key

KEY
👫 Restrooms
🍴 Food court

African Adventure

EXIT

Gift Shop

Maps have a **scale**. A scale looks like a ruler. It can be used to measure the distance between things on a map.

Maps have a **compass rose**. This feature looks like the face of a compass. It shows the **cardinal directions**. These are north, south, east, and west.

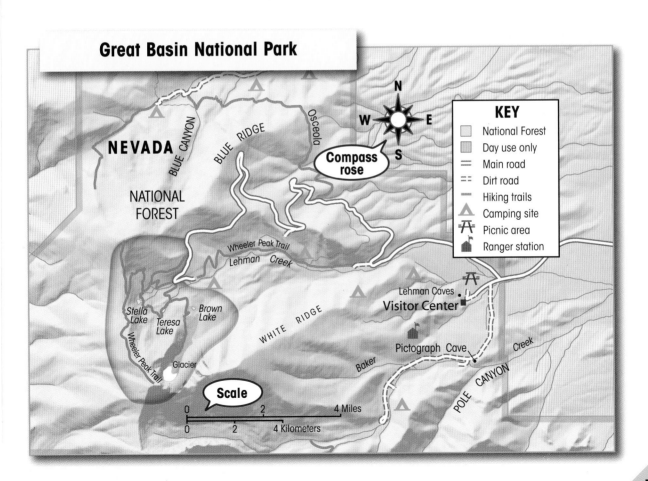

Great Basin National Park

Compass rose

Scale

KEY
- National Forest
- Day use only
- Main road
- Dirt road
- Hiking trails
- Camping site
- Picnic area
- Ranger station

NEVADA

NATIONAL FOREST

BLUE CANYON

BLUE RIDGE

Osceola

Wheeler Peak Trail

Lehman Creek

Stella Lake

Teresa Lake

Brown Lake

Wheeler Peak Trail

Glacier

WHITE RIDGE

Baker

Lehman Caves
Visitor Center

Pictograph Cave

POLE CANYON

Creek

0   2   4 Miles
0   2   4 Kilometers

Political Maps

Political maps show the location of countries. A political map of the United States shows states and their large cities. Each state is shown with a different color. Black lines show the **borders** between each state. Dots show cities, and stars show **capital** cities.

The United States of America

Olympia · WA · Salem · OR · Boise · ID · MT · Helena · ND · Bismarck · SD · Pierre · WY · Cheyenne · NE · Lincoln · Des Moines · IA · MN · St. Paul · WI · Madison · MI · Lansing · ME · Montpelier · NH · Concord · Augusta · NY · VT · Albany · MA · Boston · Hartford · Providence · RI · CT · PA · Harrisburg · Trenton · NJ · OH · Columbus · MD · Dover · DE · Annapolis · Washington DC · Sacramento · Carson City · NV · Salt Lake City · UT · CO · Denver · Topeka · KS · MO · Jefferson City · IL · Springfield · IN · Indianapolis · Frankfort · KY · WV · Charleston · VA · Richmond · CA · AZ · Phoenix · NM · Santa Fe · OK · Oklahoma City · AR · Little Rock · TN · Nashville · NC · Raleigh · SC · Columbia · GA · Atlanta · AL · Montgomery · MS · Jackson · LA · Baton Rouge · TX · Austin · Tallahassee · FL

AK · Juneau · Honolulu · HI

N · W · E · S

KEY
⊛ National capital
★ State capital

Washington D.C. is the capital of the United States.

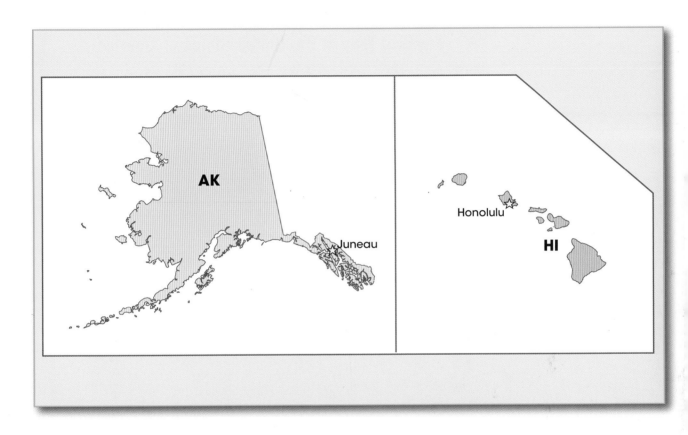

The states of Hawaii and Alaska are shown inside a box on a United States map. This is because these states are not directly connected by land to the rest of the country.

Physical Maps

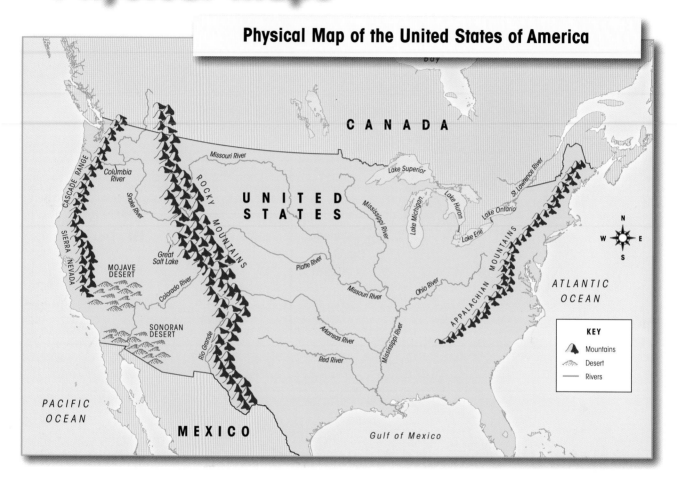

Physical Map of the United States of America

A physical map shows the natural features of the land such as mountains, lakes, and rivers. Many physical maps use **symbols** that look like these features.

Some physical maps show specific places. They show national parks, seashores, and lakeshores. The map below shows Yellowstone National Park in the western United States.

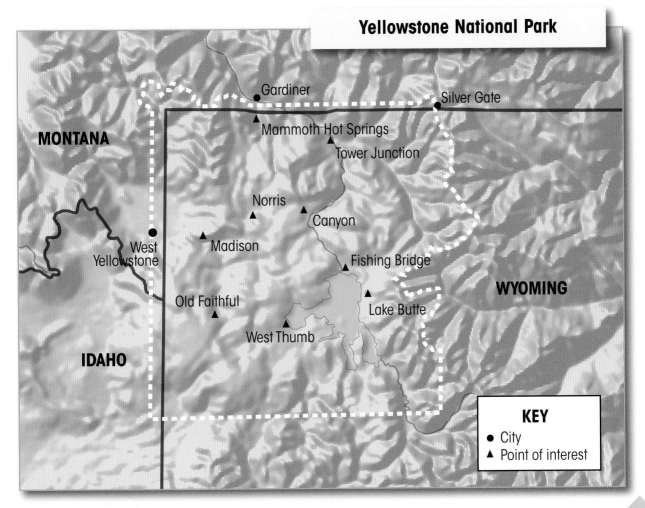

Yellowstone National Park

MONTANA

Gardiner

Silver Gate

Mammoth Hot Springs

Tower Junction

Norris

Canyon

West
Yellowstone

Madison

Fishing Bridge

WYOMING

Old Faithful

Lake Butte

West Thumb

IDAHO

KEY
● City
▲ Point of interest

Environmental Maps

Habitat maps show where a type of animal lives. A **habitat** is the natural environment of an animal or a plant. The map below shows where grizzly bears live in the western United States.

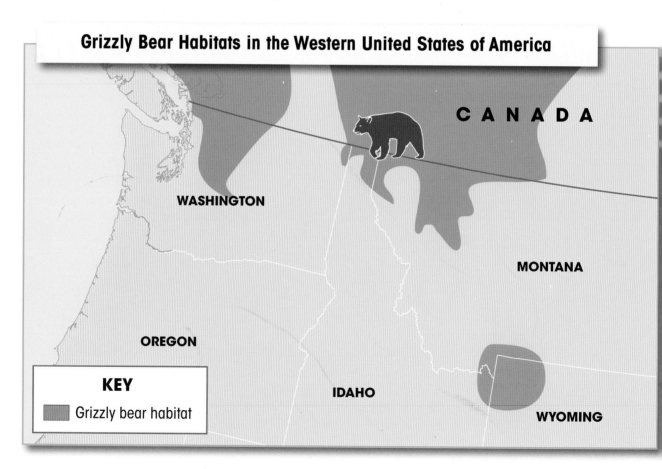

Grizzly Bear Habitats in the Western United States of America

CANADA

WASHINGTON

MONTANA

OREGON

IDAHO

WYOMING

KEY

Grizzly bear habitat

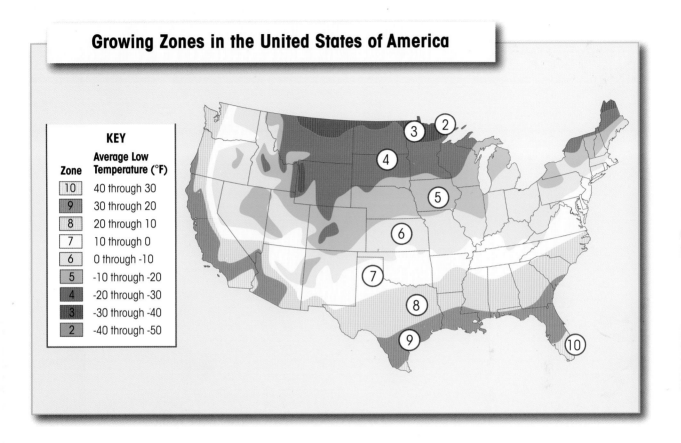

Growing Zones in the United States of America

KEY

Zone	Average Low Temperature (°F)
10	40 through 30
9	30 through 20
8	20 through 10
7	10 through 0
6	0 through -10
5	-10 through -20
4	-20 through -30
3	-30 through -40
2	-40 through -50

Some maps show where different plants grow well. Growing **zone** maps show the lowest temperature a place usually gets in a year. Farmers and gardeners can use these maps to decide what to plant. They can find out if what they want to plant can live through that low temperature.

Weather and Climate Maps

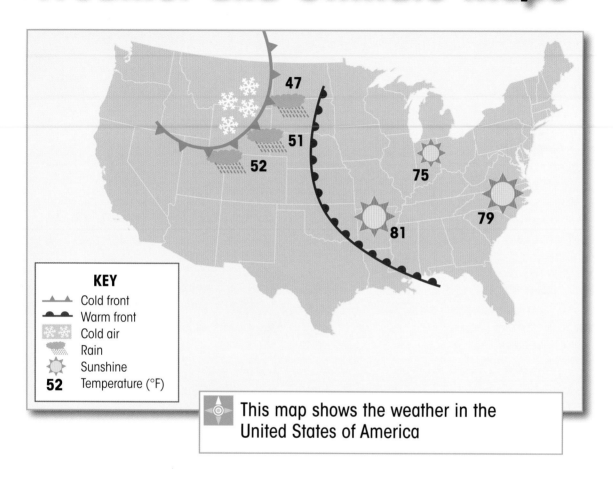

KEY
- ▲▲▲ Cold front
- ●●● Warm front
- ❄ Cold air
- ☷ Rain
- ☀ Sunshine
- **52** Temperature (°F)

This map shows the weather in the United States of America

Weather maps tell what the temperature is going to be for the day. They also show where it will be sunny or cloudy, and where it may storm. These maps have **symbols**. Some show where it will be getting colder or warmer. Others show where it will be rainy or sunny

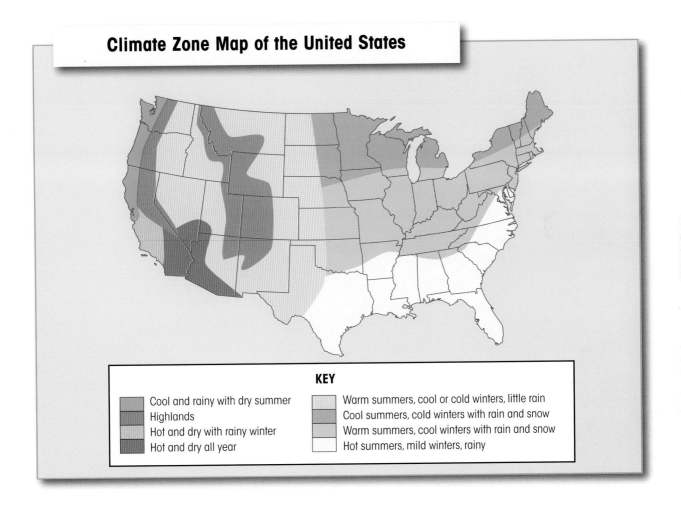

Climate Zone Map of the United States

KEY

Cool and rainy with dry summer		Warm summers, cool or cold winters, little rain	
Highlands		Cool summers, cold winters with rain and snow	
Hot and dry with rainy winter		Warm summers, cool winters with rain and snow	
Hot and dry all year		Hot summers, mild winters, rainy	

The **climate** is what the weather is usually like in an area. Climate maps use color to show different climates in an area. These areas are called climate **zones**. The United States has many different climate zones.

Road Maps

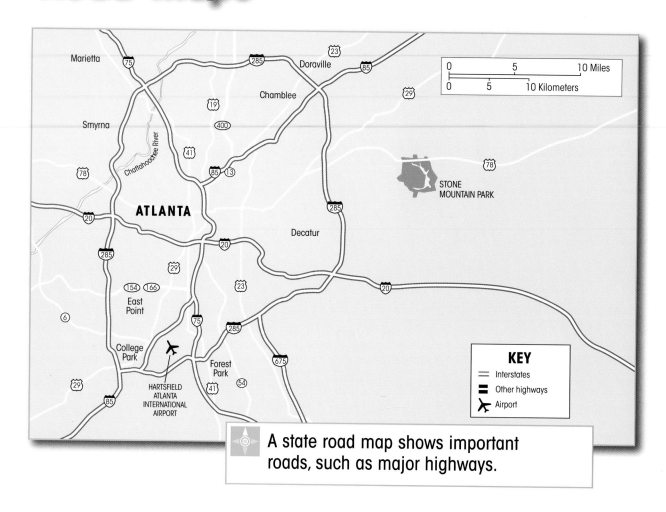

A state road map shows important roads, such as major highways.

The United States has many systems of roads. Road maps show these different roads. They help people find the best way to reach a new place.

Street maps show a smaller area than road maps. They show neighborhood streets and places of interest, such as parks and museums. Sometimes street maps and road maps are placed together in a book called a road **atlas**.

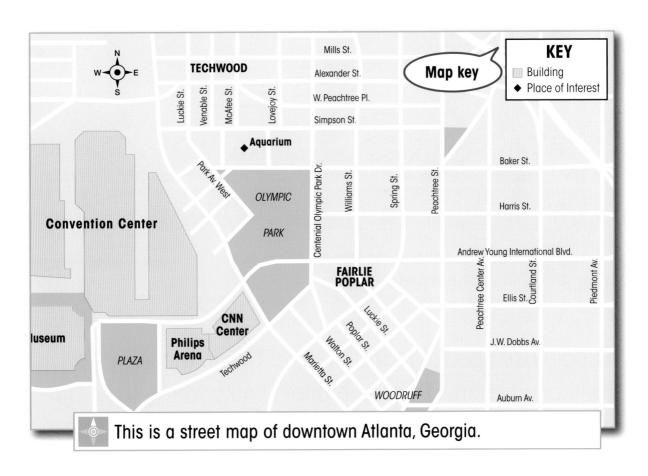

This is a street map of downtown Atlanta, Georgia.

Air and Water Maps

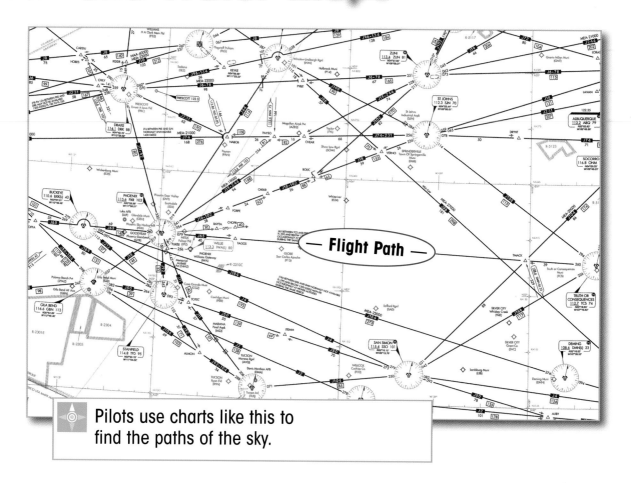

Pilots use charts like this to find the paths of the sky.

People use special maps to travel by air. These maps are called charts. They help pilots know where they are and what path to take. They also show places to avoid, such as busy areas and tall mountains.

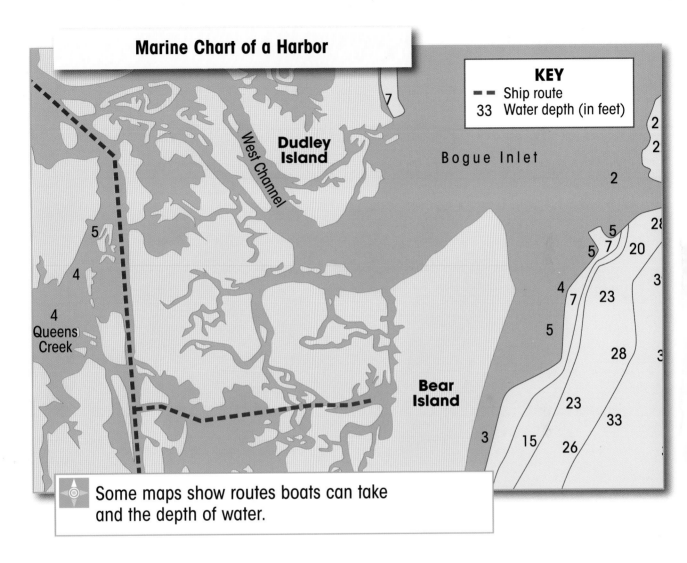

Marine Chart of a Harbor

KEY
-- Ship route
33 Water depth (in feet)

West Channel

Dudley Island

Bogue Inlet

Queens Creek

Bear Island

Some maps show routes boats can take and the depth of water.

People also use charts to travel by water. Water charts show where the water is deep and shallow. They show the location of large rocks that boats must travel around. Many water charts show safe paths that boats can use to travel.

Maps about People

Some maps tell information about people. Land-use maps show how people use the land. People use the land to farm and to graze animals. They also use the land to grow trees or make goods.

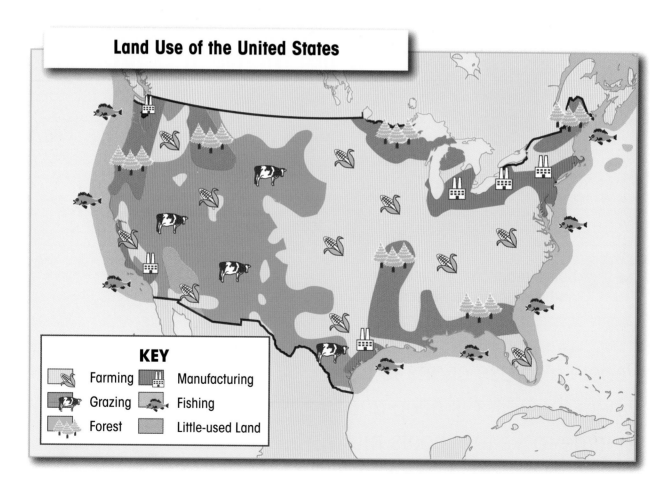

Land Use of the United States

KEY

Farming		Manufacturing	
Grazing		Fishing	
Forest		Little-used Land	

2004 U.S. Presidential Election Results

KEY
Bush states
Kerry states

Maps can show information about an event, such as an election. The map above uses color to show the results of the 2004 Presidential Election in the United States. Red is a **symbol** for states that voted for George Bush. Blue is a symbol for states that voted for John Kerry.

U.S. Census Maps

The United States **government** makes many maps about people. The government counts all the people in the country every ten years. Then it makes maps to show how many people live in an area. This is known as the U.S. **Census**.

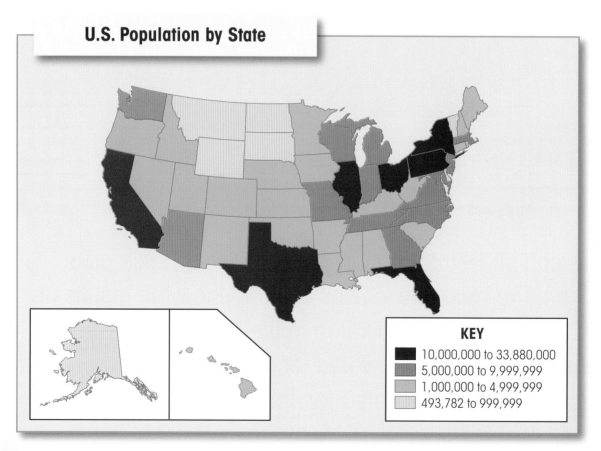

U.S. Population by State

KEY

- 10,000,000 to 33,880,000
- 5,000,000 to 9,999,999
- 1,000,000 to 4,999,999
- 493,782 to 999,999

The United States government also makes maps about businesses and farms. The map below shows the number of **acres** used to grow corn in the United States.

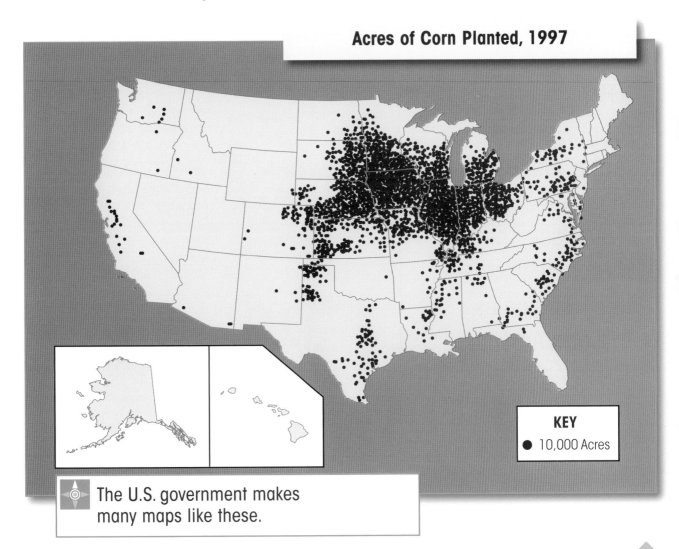

Acres of Corn Planted, 1997

KEY
● 10,000 Acres

The U.S. government makes many maps like these.

Maps about History

Maps can tell about a country's history. They can show old **borders** between countries, places where battles were fought, or paths that explorers took to reach a new place. The map here shows the 13 colonies in North America. These colonies became the first 13 states of the United States.

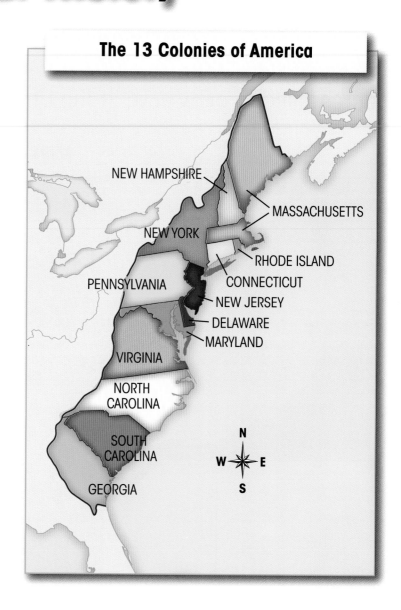

The 13 Colonies of America

NEW HAMPSHIRE

MASSACHUSETTS

NEW YORK

RHODE ISLAND

CONNECTICUT

PENNSYLVANIA

NEW JERSEY

DELAWARE

MARYLAND

VIRGINIA

NORTH CAROLINA

SOUTH CAROLINA

GEORGIA

N
W E
S

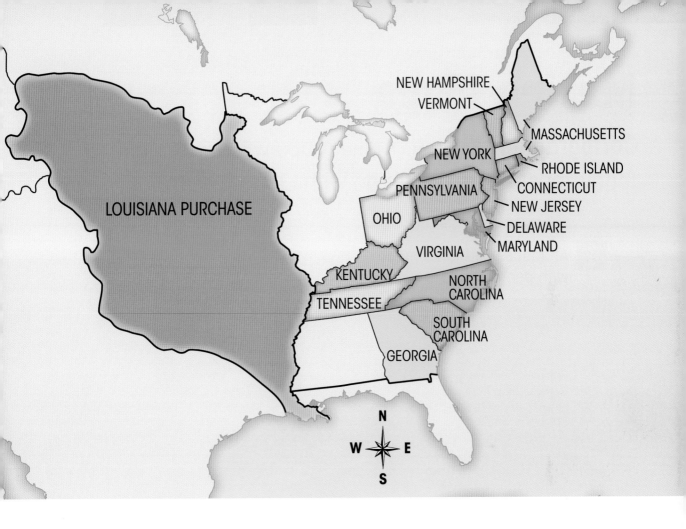

Historical maps show changes in a country. Some show when different states joined the country, or where important events took place. The map above shows when the United States bought a lot of land from the country France. This was known as the Louisiana Purchase.

Making Maps

Cartographers used to make maps with pen and ink. Today, most maps are made with computers.

All maps used to be made with pen and paper.

Today you can use a computer to view maps of areas as small as your street and as large as the world.

Computers make maps easier to use than ever. People can use the **Internet** to create road maps for travel. People can also use the Internet to see a map of their home or neighborhood.

No matter how maps are made, they can help you learn many things about your country.

Map Activities

Activity 1
Map Collection

Look through a newspaper and cut out every map
you see. Do this every day for one week. Make sure
you get permission from an adult. At the end of the
week, compare the maps. What types of information
do they show? How are the maps different from
each other? If you cannot get a paper that you are
allowed to cut, use the **Internet** version of your
local newspaper.

Activity 2
Create Your Own Census Map

You can create a **census** map of your classroom.
Pick a question to ask your classmates, such as "Do
you have a pet?" or "What is your favorite color?"
Draw a map of your classroom, including where
people sit and that includes this information.

Assign a color to each answer for your question. For example, if your question was "Do you have any brothers or sisters?" you might pick red for "yes" and green for "no." On the map, put the correct color dot to each desk.

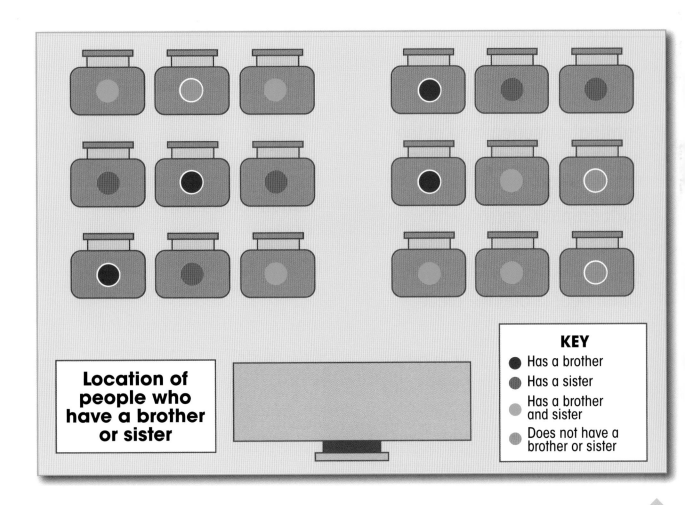

Location of people who have a brother or sister

KEY
- Has a brother
- Has a sister
- Has a brother and sister
- Does not have a brother or sister

Glossary

acre unit of area used to measure land about the size of a football field

atlas collection of maps in a book

border imaginary line that divides two places

capital city where leaders of a state or country meet and work

cardinal direction one of the four main directions: north, south, east, or west

cartographer person who makes maps

census collection of information about people and the place where they live

climate usual weather in an area. The weather changes from day to day, but the climate stays the same.

compass rose symbol on a map that shows direction

government group of people who make decisions about how to run a city, state, or country

habitat natural environment and the plants and animals that live there

Internet computer network people use for email and for getting information from many sources around the world

key table that shows what the symbols on a map mean

population group or number of people

scale feature on a map that can be used to measure distance

symbol picture that stands for something else

zone area that has something in common

Find Out More

Organizations and Websites

The Websites below may have some advertisements on them. Make sure to ask a trusted adult to look at them with you. You should never give out personal information, including your name and address, without talking to a trusted adult.

American Automobile Association (AAA)
AAA is a group of related automobile clubs. AAA clubs provide free map and direction services to members. Visit **www.aaa.com** to find a AAA club near you, or put AAA and your state name into a trusted search engine.

National Geographic
National Geographic provides free maps and photos of the Earth, as well as interesting articles about people and animals. Visit **www.nationalgeographic.com**.

U.S. Census Bureau
The U.S. Census Bureau has a lot of interesting information about the people of the United States. The website even allows you to create your own maps based on the information. The website is made for adults, so you may need some help getting the information you want. Visit **www.census.gov**.

Yahoo Maps
Find directions from your house to places nearby and far away. Try putting in your address and the address of your school. Do the directions given match your route?
www.maps.yahoo.com

Books to Read

Baber, Maxwell. *Map Basics*. Chicago: Heinemann Library, 2007.

Hooke, R. Schuyler. *X Marks the Spot*. New York: Random House, 2007.

Mahaney, Ian F. *Political Maps*. New York: Rosen, 2007.

Index

acre 23
atlas 17

border 8, 24

capital 8
cardinal direction 7
cartographer 4, 26
census 22, 28
climate 14, 15
compass rose 7, 17

government 22, 23

habitat 12

Internet 27, 28

key 6-8, 10, 13-17, 19- 23, 29

lake 4, 7, 10, 11

ocean 21

population 22

scale 7
state 5, 8, 9, 11-13, 15, 16,
    20-25

symbol 6, 10, 14, 21

zone 13, 15